YouTube
PLANNER

NAME: _____

PHONE: _____

2021
CALENDAR

JANUARY

Mon	Tue	Wed	Thu	Fri	Sat	Sun
				1	2	3
4	5	6	7	8	9	10
11	12	13	14	15	16	17
18	19	20	21	22	23	24
25	26	27	28	29	30	31

FEBRUARY

Mon	Tue	Wed	Thu	Fri	Sat	Sun
1	2	3	4	5	6	7
8	9	10	11	12	13	14
15	16	17	18	19	20	21
22	23	24	25	26	27	28

MARCH

Mon	Tue	Wed	Thu	Fri	Sat	Sun
1	2	3	4	5	6	7
8	9	10	11	12	13	14
15	16	17	18	19	20	21
22	23	24	25	26	27	28
29	30	31				

APRIL

Mon	Tue	Wed	Thu	Fri	Sat	Sun
			1	2	3	4
5	6	7	8	9	10	11
12	13	14	15	16	17	18
19	20	21	22	23	24	25
26	27	28	29	30		

MAY

Mon	Tue	Wed	Thu	Fri	Sat	Sun
					1	2
3	4	5	6	7	8	9
10	11	12	13	14	15	16
17	18	19	20	21	22	23
24/31	25	26	27	28	29	30

JUNE

Mon	Tue	Wed	Thu	Fri	Sat	Sun
	1	2	3	4	5	6
7	8	9	10	11	12	13
14	15	16	17	18	19	20
21	22	23	24	25	26	27
28	29	30				

JULY

Mon	Tue	Wed	Thu	Fri	Sat	Sun
			1	2	3	4
5	6	7	8	9	10	11
12	13	14	15	16	17	18
19	20	21	22	23	24	25
26	27	28	29	30	31	

AUGUST

Mon	Tue	Wed	Thu	Fri	Sat	Sun
						1
2	3	4	5	6	7	8
9	10	11	12	13	14	15
16	17	18	19	20	21	22
23/30	24/31	25	26	27	28	29

SEPTEMBER

Mon	Tue	Wed	Thu	Fri	Sat	Sun
		1	2	3	4	5
6	7	8	9	10	11	12
13	14	15	16	17	18	19
20	21	22	23	24	25	26
27	28	29	30			

OCTOBER

Mon	Tue	Wed	Thu	Fri	Sat	Sun
				1	2	3
4	5	6	7	8	9	10
11	12	13	14	15	16	17
18	19	20	21	22	23	24
25	26	27	28	29	30	31

NOVEMBER

Mon	Tue	Wed	Thu	Fri	Sat	Sun
1	2	3	4	5	6	7
8	9	10	11	12	13	14
15	16	17	18	19	20	21
22	23	24	25	26	27	28
29	30					

DECEMBER

Mon	Tue	Wed	Thu	Fri	Sat	Sun
		1	2	3	4	5
6	7	8	9	10	11	12
13	14	15	16	17	18	19
20	21	22	23	24	25	26
27	28	29	30	31		

2022
CALENDAR

JANUARY

Mon	Tue	Wed	Thu	Fri	Sat	Sun
					1	2
3	4	5	6	7	8	9
10	11	12	13	14	15	16
17	18	19	20	21	22	23
24/31	25	26	27	28	29	30

FEBRUARY

Mon	Tue	Wed	Thu	Fri	Sat	Sun
	1	2	3	4	5	6
7	8	9	10	11	12	13
14	15	16	17	18	19	20
21	22	23	24	25	26	27
28						

MARCH

Mon	Tue	Wed	Thu	Fri	Sat	Sun
	1	2	3	4	5	6
7	8	9	10	11	12	13
14	15	16	17	18	19	20
21	22	23	24	25	26	27
28	29	30	31			

APRIL

Mon	Tue	Wed	Thu	Fri	Sat	Sun
				1	2	3
4	5	6	7	8	9	10
11	12	13	14	15	16	17
18	19	20	21	22	23	24
25	26	27	28	29	30	

MAY

Mon	Tue	Wed	Thu	Fri	Sat	Sun
						1
2	3	4	5	6	7	8
9	10	11	12	13	14	15
16	17	18	19	20	21	22
23/30	24/31	25	26	27	28	29

JUNE

Mon	Tue	Wed	Thu	Fri	Sat	Sun
		1	2	3	4	5
6	7	8	9	10	11	12
13	14	15	16	17	18	19
20	21	22	23	24	25	26
27	28	29	30			

JULY

Mon	Tue	Wed	Thu	Fri	Sat	Sun
				1	2	3
4	5	6	7	8	9	10
11	12	13	14	15	16	17
18	19	20	21	22	23	24
25	26	27	28	29	30	31

AUGUST

Mon	Tue	Wed	Thu	Fri	Sat	Sun
1	2	3	4	5	6	7
8	9	10	11	12	13	14
15	16	17	18	19	20	21
22	23	24	25	26	27	28
29	30	31				

SEPTEMBER

Mon	Tue	Wed	Thu	Fri	Sat	Sun
			1	2	3	4
5	6	7	8	9	10	11
12	13	14	15	16	17	18
19	20	21	22	23	24	25
26	27	28	29	30		

OCTOBER

Mon	Tue	Wed	Thu	Fri	Sat	Sun
					1	2
3	4	5	6	7	8	9
10	11	12	13	14	15	16
17	18	19	20	21	22	23
24/31	25	26	27	28	29	30

NOVEMBER

Mon	Tue	Wed	Thu	Fri	Sat	Sun
	1	2	3	4	5	6
7	8	9	10	11	12	13
14	15	16	17	18	19	20
21	22	23	24	25	26	27
28	29	30				

DECEMBER

Mon	Tue	Wed	Thu	Fri	Sat	Sun
			1	2	3	4
5	6	7	8	9	10	11
12	13	14	15	16	17	18
19	20	21	22	23	24	25
26	27	28	29	30	31	

YouTube *Planner*

VIDEO TITLE	Cyberpunk	CATEGORY	Gaming	DURATION	
KEYWORDS	cyberpunk, chat, guys, how your day follow	📅		🕐 15 minutes	

DESCRIPTION
Testing out new game cyberpunk and showing the game

SUPPLIES
Chromebook
mic
Ring light

CHECKLIST
- ✓ 🎥 FILM
- ✓ 🎤 VOICEOVER
- ☐ 📝 EDIT
- ✓ 🖼 THUMBNAIL
- ✓ 📄 DESCRIPTION
- ☐ 🏷 TAG
- ✓ ⬆ UPLOAD
- ☐ ✨ EFFECTS
- ☐ 🎵 MUSIC
- ☐ 🎉 POSTED

TALK ABOUT
- ☐ how the game is new
- ☐ learn with me
- ☐ make sure to follow
- ☐ later streams
- ☐ how I try stream daily

SOCIAL MEDIA
- ☐ ✉ ✓ 📷 ☐ f
- ☐ 🐦 ☐ P ☐ W

@eatthetash   tk30_vilson

LINKS

YouTube *Planner*

VIDEO TITLE

CATEGORY

DURATION

KEYWORDS

DESCRIPTION

SUPPLIES

CHECKLIST

- ☐ FILM
- ☐ VOICEOVER
- ☐ EDIT
- ☐ THUMBNAIL
- ☐ DESCRIPTION
- ☐ TAG
- ☐ UPLOAD
- ☐ EFFECTS
- ☐ MUSIC
- ☐ POSTED

TALK ABOUT

☐
☐
☐
☐
☐
☐
☐
☐
☐
☐
☐

SOCIAL MEDIA

- ☐ ✉
- ☐ Instagram
- ☐ Facebook
- ☐ Twitter
- ☐ Pinterest
- ☐ WordPress

LINKS

YouTube *Planner*

VIDEO TITLE

CATEGORY

DURATION

KEYWORDS

DESCRIPTION

SUPPLIES

CHECKLIST

TALK ABOUT

- ☐ 🎥 FILM
- ☐ 🎤 VOICEOVER
- ☐ 📝 EDIT
- ☐ 🖼 THUMBNAIL
- ☐ 📄 DESCRIPTION
- ☐ 🏷 TAG
- ☐ ⬆ UPLOAD
- ☐ ✨ EFFECTS
- ☐ 🎵 MUSIC
- ☐ 🎉 POSTED

SOCIAL MEDIA

- ☐ ✉
- ☐ 📷
- ☐ f
- ☐ 🐦
- ☐ P
- ☐ W

LINKS

YouTube *Planner*

VIDEO TITLE | **CATEGORY** | **DURATION**

KEYWORDS

DESCRIPTION

SUPPLIES

CHECKLIST

- ☐ 🎥 FILM
- ☐ 🎤 VOICEOVER
- ☐ 📝 EDIT
- ☐ 🖼 THUMBNAIL
- ☐ 📄 DESCRIPTION
- ☐ 🏷 TAG
- ☐ ⬆ UPLOAD
- ☐ ✨ EFFECTS
- ☐ 🎵 MUSIC
- ☐ 🎉 POSTED

TALK ABOUT

SOCIAL MEDIA

- ☐ ✉
- ☐ 📷
- ☐ f
- ☐ 🐦
- ☐ P
- ☐ W

LINKS

YouTube *Planner*

VIDEO TITLE	CATEGORY	DURATION
KEYWORDS		

DESCRIPTION

SUPPLIES

CHECKLIST

- ☐ FILM
- ☐ VOICEOVER
- ☐ EDIT
- ☐ THUMBNAIL
- ☐ DESCRIPTION
- ☐ TAG
- ☐ UPLOAD
- ☐ EFFECTS
- ☐ MUSIC
- ☐ POSTED

TALK ABOUT

SOCIAL MEDIA

- ☐ ✉
- ☐ Instagram
- ☐ Facebook
- ☐ Twitter
- ☐ Pinterest
- ☐ WordPress

LINKS

YouTube *Planner*

VIDEO TITLE	CATEGORY	DURATION
KEYWORDS	📅	🕒

DESCRIPTION

SUPPLIES

CHECKLIST

- ☐ 🎥 FILM
- ☐ 🎤 VOICEOVER
- ☐ 📝 EDIT
- ☐ 🖼 THUMBNAIL
- ☐ 📄 DESCRIPTION
- ☐ 🏷 TAG
- ☐ ⬆ UPLOAD
- ☐ ✨ EFFECTS
- ☐ 🎵 MUSIC
- ☐ 🎉 POSTED

TALK ABOUT

- ☐
- ☐
- ☐
- ☐
- ☐
- ☐
- ☐
- ☐
- ☐
- ☐
- ☐

SOCIAL MEDIA

- ☐ ✉
- ☐ 📷 Instagram
- ☐ f Facebook
- ☐ 🐦 Twitter
- ☐ P Pinterest
- ☐ W WordPress

LINKS

YouTube *Planner*

VIDEO TITLE

CATEGORY

DURATION

KEYWORDS

DESCRIPTION

SUPPLIES

CHECKLIST

- [ ] FILM
- [ ] VOICEOVER
- [ ] EDIT
- [ ] THUMBNAIL
- [ ] DESCRIPTION
- [ ] TAG
- [ ] UPLOAD
- [ ] EFFECTS
- [ ] MUSIC
- [ ] POSTED

TALK ABOUT

SOCIAL MEDIA

- [ ] ✉
- [ ] Instagram
- [ ] Facebook
- [ ] Twitter
- [ ] Pinterest
- [ ] WordPress

LINKS

YouTube *Planner*

VIDEO TITLE

CATEGORY

DURATION

KEYWORDS

DESCRIPTION

SUPPLIES

CHECKLIST

- [ ] FILM
- [ ] VOICEOVER
- [ ] EDIT
- [ ] THUMBNAIL
- [ ] DESCRIPTION
- [ ] TAG
- [ ] UPLOAD
- [ ] EFFECTS
- [ ] MUSIC
- [ ] POSTED

TALK ABOUT

- [ ]
- [ ]
- [ ]
- [ ]
- [ ]
- [ ]
- [ ]
- [ ]
- [ ]
- [ ]
- [ ]

SOCIAL MEDIA

- [ ] ✉
- [ ] Instagram
- [ ] Facebook
- [ ] Twitter
- [ ] Pinterest
- [ ] WordPress

LINKS

YouTube *Planner*

VIDEO TITLE

CATEGORY

DURATION

KEYWORDS

DESCRIPTION

SUPPLIES

CHECKLIST

- ☐ 🎥 FILM
- ☐ 🎤 VOICEOVER
- ☐ 📝 EDIT
- ☐ 🖼 THUMBNAIL
- ☐ 📄 DESCRIPTION
- ☐ 🏷 TAG
- ☐ 📤 UPLOAD
- ☐ ✨ EFFECTS
- ☐ 🎵 MUSIC
- ☐ 🎉 POSTED

TALK ABOUT

- ☐
- ☐
- ☐
- ☐
- ☐
- ☐
- ☐
- ☐
- ☐
- ☐

SOCIAL MEDIA

- ☐ ✉
- ☐ 📷
- ☐ f
- ☐ 🐦
- ☐ P
- ☐ W

LINKS

YouTube *Planner*

VIDEO TITLE	CATEGORY	DURATION
KEYWORDS	📅	🕐

DESCRIPTION

SUPPLIES

CHECKLIST

- ☐ 🎥 FILM
- ☐ 🎤 VOICEOVER
- ☐ 📝 EDIT
- ☐ 🖼 THUMBNAIL
- ☐ 📄 DESCRIPTION
- ☐ 🏷 TAG
- ☐ ⬆ UPLOAD
- ☐ ✨ EFFECTS
- ☐ 🎵 MUSIC
- ☐ 🎉 POSTED

TALK ABOUT

- ☐
- ☐
- ☐
- ☐
- ☐
- ☐
- ☐
- ☐
- ☐
- ☐
- ☐
- ☐

SOCIAL MEDIA

- ☐ ✉
- ☐ 📷
- ☐ f
- ☐ 🐦
- ☐ ⓟ
- ☐ Ⓦ

LINKS

YouTube *Planner*

| VIDEO TITLE | CATEGORY | DURATION |

KEYWORDS

DESCRIPTION

SUPPLIES

CHECKLIST

- [ ] FILM
- [ ] VOICEOVER
- [ ] EDIT
- [ ] THUMBNAIL
- [ ] DESCRIPTION
- [ ] TAG
- [ ] UPLOAD
- [ ] EFFECTS
- [ ] MUSIC
- [ ] POSTED

TALK ABOUT

- [ ]
- [ ]
- [ ]
- [ ]
- [ ]
- [ ]
- [ ]
- [ ]
- [ ]
- [ ]
- [ ]

SOCIAL MEDIA

- [ ] ✉
- [ ] Instagram
- [ ] Facebook
- [ ] Twitter
- [ ] Pinterest
- [ ] WordPress

LINKS

YouTube *Planner*

VIDEO TITLE

CATEGORY

DURATION

KEYWORDS

DESCRIPTION

SUPPLIES

CHECKLIST

- [ ] FILM
- [ ] VOICEOVER
- [ ] EDIT
- [ ] THUMBNAIL
- [ ] DESCRIPTION
- [ ] TAG
- [ ] UPLOAD
- [ ] EFFECTS
- [ ] MUSIC
- [ ] POSTED

TALK ABOUT

- [ ]
- [ ]
- [ ]
- [ ]
- [ ]
- [ ]
- [ ]
- [ ]
- [ ]
- [ ]
- [ ]
- [ ]

SOCIAL MEDIA

- [ ] ✉
- [ ] Instagram
- [ ] Facebook
- [ ] Twitter
- [ ] Pinterest
- [ ] WordPress

LINKS

YouTube *Planner*

| VIDEO TITLE | CATEGORY | DURATION |

KEYWORDS

DESCRIPTION

SUPPLIES

CHECKLIST

- ☐ 🎥 FILM
- ☐ 🎤 VOICEOVER
- ☐ 📝 EDIT
- ☐ 🖼 THUMBNAIL
- ☐ 📄 DESCRIPTION
- ☐ 🏷 TAG
- ☐ ⬆ UPLOAD
- ☐ ✨ EFFECTS
- ☐ 🎵 MUSIC
- ☐ 🎉 POSTED

TALK ABOUT

☐
☐
☐
☐
☐
☐
☐
☐
☐
☐
☐

SOCIAL MEDIA

- ☐ ✉
- ☐ 📷
- ☐ f
- ☐ 🐦
- ☐ P
- ☐ W

LINKS

YouTube *Planner*

VIDEO TITLE	CATEGORY	DURATION
KEYWORDS		

DESCRIPTION

SUPPLIES

CHECKLIST

- ☐ FILM
- ☐ VOICEOVER
- ☐ EDIT
- ☐ THUMBNAIL
- ☐ DESCRIPTION
- ☐ TAG
- ☐ UPLOAD
- ☐ EFFECTS
- ☐ MUSIC
- ☐ POSTED

TALK ABOUT

☐
☐
☐
☐
☐
☐
☐
☐
☐
☐
☐

SOCIAL MEDIA

- ☐ ✉
- ☐ Instagram
- ☐ Facebook
- ☐ Twitter
- ☐ Pinterest
- ☐ WordPress

LINKS

YouTube *Planner*

VIDEO TITLE

CATEGORY

DURATION

KEYWORDS

DESCRIPTION

SUPPLIES

CHECKLIST

- ☐ FILM
- ☐ VOICEOVER
- ☐ EDIT
- ☐ THUMBNAIL
- ☐ DESCRIPTION
- ☐ TAG
- ☐ UPLOAD
- ☐ EFFECTS
- ☐ MUSIC
- ☐ POSTED

TALK ABOUT

SOCIAL MEDIA

- ☐ ✉
- ☐ Instagram
- ☐ Facebook
- ☐ Twitter
- ☐ Pinterest
- ☐ WordPress

LINKS

YouTube *Planner*

| VIDEO TITLE | CATEGORY | DURATION |

KEYWORDS

DESCRIPTION

SUPPLIES

CHECKLIST

- [ ] FILM
- [ ] VOICEOVER
- [ ] EDIT
- [ ] THUMBNAIL
- [ ] DESCRIPTION
- [ ] TAG
- [ ] UPLOAD
- [ ] EFFECTS
- [ ] MUSIC
- [ ] POSTED

TALK ABOUT

SOCIAL MEDIA

- [ ] ✉
- [ ] Instagram
- [ ] Facebook
- [ ] Twitter
- [ ] Pinterest
- [ ] WordPress

LINKS

YouTube *Planner*

VIDEO TITLE	CATEGORY	DURATION
KEYWORDS		

DESCRIPTION

SUPPLIES

CHECKLIST

- ☐ 🎥 FILM
- ☐ 🎤 VOICEOVER
- ☐ 📝 EDIT
- ☐ 🖼 THUMBNAIL
- ☐ 📄 DESCRIPTION
- ☐ 🏷 TAG
- ☐ ⬆ UPLOAD
- ☐ ✨ EFFECTS
- ☐ 🎵 MUSIC
- ☐ 🎉 POSTED

TALK ABOUT

- ☐
- ☐
- ☐
- ☐
- ☐
- ☐
- ☐
- ☐
- ☐
- ☐
- ☐

SOCIAL MEDIA

- ☐ ✉
- ☐ 📷
- ☐ f
- ☐ 🐦
- ☐ P
- ☐ W

LINKS

YouTube *Planner*

VIDEO TITLE

CATEGORY

DURATION

KEYWORDS

DESCRIPTION

SUPPLIES

CHECKLIST

- ☐ FILM
- ☐ VOICEOVER
- ☐ EDIT
- ☐ THUMBNAIL
- ☐ DESCRIPTION
- ☐ TAG
- ☐ UPLOAD
- ☐ EFFECTS
- ☐ MUSIC
- ☐ POSTED

TALK ABOUT

SOCIAL MEDIA

LINKS

YouTube *Planner*

| VIDEO TITLE | CATEGORY | DURATION |

| KEYWORDS | | |

DESCRIPTION

SUPPLIES

CHECKLIST

- ☐ FILM
- ☐ VOICEOVER
- ☐ EDIT
- ☐ THUMBNAIL
- ☐ DESCRIPTION
- ☐ TAG
- ☐ UPLOAD
- ☐ EFFECTS
- ☐ MUSIC
- ☐ POSTED

TALK ABOUT

SOCIAL MEDIA

- ☐ ✉
- ☐ Instagram
- ☐ Facebook
- ☐ Twitter
- ☐ Pinterest
- ☐ WordPress

LINKS

YouTube *Planner*

VIDEO TITLE

CATEGORY

DURATION

KEYWORDS

DESCRIPTION

SUPPLIES

CHECKLIST

- ☐ FILM
- ☐ VOICEOVER
- ☐ EDIT
- ☐ THUMBNAIL
- ☐ DESCRIPTION
- ☐ TAG
- ☐ UPLOAD
- ☐ EFFECTS
- ☐ MUSIC
- ☐ POSTED

TALK ABOUT

- ☐
- ☐
- ☐
- ☐
- ☐
- ☐
- ☐
- ☐
- ☐
- ☐
- ☐

SOCIAL MEDIA

- ☐ ✉
- ☐ 🐦
- ☐ Instagram
- ☐ Pinterest
- ☐ Facebook
- ☐ WordPress

LINKS

YouTube *Planner*

| VIDEO TITLE | CATEGORY | DURATION |
| KEYWORDS | | |

DESCRIPTION

SUPPLIES

CHECKLIST

- ☐ FILM
- ☐ VOICEOVER
- ☐ EDIT
- ☐ THUMBNAIL
- ☐ DESCRIPTION
- ☐ TAG
- ☐ UPLOAD
- ☐ EFFECTS
- ☐ MUSIC
- ☐ POSTED

TALK ABOUT

☐
☐
☐
☐
☐
☐
☐
☐
☐
☐
☐

SOCIAL MEDIA

- ☐ ✉
- ☐ Instagram
- ☐ Facebook
- ☐ Twitter
- ☐ Pinterest
- ☐ WordPress

LINKS

YouTube *Planner*

VIDEO TITLE

CATEGORY

DURATION

KEYWORDS

DESCRIPTION

SUPPLIES

CHECKLIST

- ☐ FILM
- ☐ VOICEOVER
- ☐ EDIT
- ☐ THUMBNAIL
- ☐ DESCRIPTION
- ☐ TAG
- ☐ UPLOAD
- ☐ EFFECTS
- ☐ MUSIC
- ☐ POSTED

TALK ABOUT

SOCIAL MEDIA

- ☐ ✉
- ☐ Instagram
- ☐ Facebook
- ☐ Twitter
- ☐ Pinterest
- ☐ WordPress

LINKS

YouTube *Planner*

VIDEO TITLE | **CATEGORY** | **DURATION**

KEYWORDS

DESCRIPTION

SUPPLIES

CHECKLIST

- ☐ FILM
- ☐ VOICEOVER
- ☐ EDIT
- ☐ THUMBNAIL
- ☐ DESCRIPTION
- ☐ TAG
- ☐ UPLOAD
- ☐ EFFECTS
- ☐ MUSIC
- ☐ POSTED

TALK ABOUT

SOCIAL MEDIA

- ☐ Email
- ☐ Instagram
- ☐ Facebook
- ☐ Twitter
- ☐ Pinterest
- ☐ WordPress

LINKS

YouTube *Planner*

VIDEO TITLE	CATEGORY	DURATION
KEYWORDS	📅	🕐

DESCRIPTION

SUPPLIES

CHECKLIST

- ☐ 🎥 FILM
- ☐ 🎤 VOICEOVER
- ☐ 📝 EDIT
- ☐ 🖼 THUMBNAIL
- ☐ 📄 DESCRIPTION
- ☐ 🏷 TAG
- ☐ ⬆ UPLOAD
- ☐ ✨ EFFECTS
- ☐ 🎵 MUSIC
- ☐ 🎉 POSTED

TALK ABOUT

- ☐
- ☐
- ☐
- ☐
- ☐
- ☐
- ☐
- ☐
- ☐
- ☐
- ☐
- ☐

SOCIAL MEDIA

- ☐ ✉
- ☐ 🐦
- ☐ 📷
- ☐ 📌
- ☐ f
- ☐ W

LINKS

YouTube *Planner*

VIDEO TITLE | **CATEGORY** | **DURATION**

KEYWORDS

DESCRIPTION

SUPPLIES

CHECKLIST

- ☐ 🎥 FILM
- ☐ 🎤 VOICEOVER
- ☐ 📝 EDIT
- ☐ 🖼 THUMBNAIL
- ☐ 📄 DESCRIPTION
- ☐ 🏷 TAG
- ☐ ⬆ UPLOAD
- ☐ ✨ EFFECTS
- ☐ 🎵 MUSIC
- ☐ 🎉 POSTED

TALK ABOUT

- ☐
- ☐
- ☐
- ☐
- ☐
- ☐
- ☐
- ☐
- ☐
- ☐
- ☐
- ☐

SOCIAL MEDIA

- ☐ ✉
- ☐ 📷
- ☐ f
- ☐ 🐦
- ☐ P
- ☐ W

LINKS

YouTube *Planner*

VIDEO TITLE	CATEGORY	DURATION
KEYWORDS	📅	🕐

DESCRIPTION

SUPPLIES

CHECKLIST

- ☐ 🎥 FILM
- ☐ 🎤 VOICEOVER
- ☐ 📝 EDIT
- ☐ 🖼 THUMBNAIL
- ☐ 📄 DESCRIPTION
- ☐ 🏷 TAG
- ☐ ⬆ UPLOAD
- ☐ ✨ EFFECTS
- ☐ 🎵 MUSIC
- ☐ 🎉 POSTED

TALK ABOUT

☐
☐
☐
☐
☐
☐
☐
☐
☐
☐
☐

SOCIAL MEDIA

- ☐ ✉
- ☐ 📷
- ☐ f
- ☐ 🐦
- ☐ 𝓟
- ☐ W

LINKS

YouTube *Planner*

| VIDEO TITLE | CATEGORY | DURATION |

KEYWORDS

DESCRIPTION

SUPPLIES

CHECKLIST

- ☐ 🎥 FILM
- ☐ 🎤 VOICEOVER
- ☐ 📝 EDIT
- ☐ 🖼 THUMBNAIL
- ☐ 📄 DESCRIPTION
- ☐ 🏷 TAG
- ☐ ⬆ UPLOAD
- ☐ ✨ EFFECTS
- ☐ 🎵 MUSIC
- ☐ 🎉 POSTED

TALK ABOUT

☐
☐
☐
☐
☐
☐
☐
☐
☐
☐
☐

SOCIAL MEDIA

- ☐ ✉
- ☐ 📷
- ☐ f
- ☐ 🐦
- ☐ P
- ☐ W

LINKS

YouTube *Planner*

| VIDEO TITLE | CATEGORY | DURATION |

KEYWORDS

DESCRIPTION

SUPPLIES

CHECKLIST

- ☐ FILM
- ☐ VOICEOVER
- ☐ EDIT
- ☐ THUMBNAIL
- ☐ DESCRIPTION
- ☐ TAG
- ☐ UPLOAD
- ☐ EFFECTS
- ☐ MUSIC
- ☐ POSTED

TALK ABOUT

SOCIAL MEDIA

- ☐ ✉
- ☐ Instagram
- ☐ Facebook
- ☐ Twitter
- ☐ Pinterest
- ☐ WordPress

LINKS

YouTube *Planner*

| VIDEO TITLE | CATEGORY | DURATION |

KEYWORDS

DESCRIPTION

SUPPLIES

CHECKLIST

- ☐ FILM
- ☐ VOICEOVER
- ☐ EDIT
- ☐ THUMBNAIL
- ☐ DESCRIPTION
- ☐ TAG
- ☐ UPLOAD
- ☐ EFFECTS
- ☐ MUSIC
- ☐ POSTED

TALK ABOUT

SOCIAL MEDIA

- ☐ ✉
- ☐ Instagram
- ☐ Facebook
- ☐ Twitter
- ☐ Pinterest
- ☐ WordPress

LINKS

YouTube *Planner*

VIDEO TITLE	CATEGORY	DURATION
KEYWORDS		

DESCRIPTION

SUPPLIES

CHECKLIST

- [ ] FILM
- [ ] VOICEOVER
- [ ] EDIT
- [ ] THUMBNAIL
- [ ] DESCRIPTION
- [ ] TAG
- [ ] UPLOAD
- [ ] EFFECTS
- [ ] MUSIC
- [ ] POSTED

TALK ABOUT

- [ ]
- [ ]
- [ ]
- [ ]
- [ ]
- [ ]
- [ ]
- [ ]
- [ ]
- [ ]
- [ ]
- [ ]

SOCIAL MEDIA

- [ ] ✉
- [ ] Instagram
- [ ] Facebook
- [ ] Twitter
- [ ] Pinterest
- [ ] WordPress

LINKS

YouTube *Planner*

VIDEO TITLE | **CATEGORY** | **DURATION**

KEYWORDS

DESCRIPTION

SUPPLIES

CHECKLIST

- [ ] FILM
- [ ] VOICEOVER
- [ ] EDIT
- [ ] THUMBNAIL
- [ ] DESCRIPTION
- [ ] TAG
- [ ] UPLOAD
- [ ] EFFECTS
- [ ] MUSIC
- [ ] POSTED

TALK ABOUT

SOCIAL MEDIA

LINKS

YouTube *Planner*

VIDEO TITLE

CATEGORY

DURATION

KEYWORDS

DESCRIPTION

SUPPLIES

CHECKLIST

- ☐ FILM
- ☐ VOICEOVER
- ☐ EDIT
- ☐ THUMBNAIL
- ☐ DESCRIPTION
- ☐ TAG
- ☐ UPLOAD
- ☐ EFFECTS
- ☐ MUSIC
- ☐ POSTED

TALK ABOUT

- ☐
- ☐
- ☐
- ☐
- ☐
- ☐
- ☐
- ☐
- ☐
- ☐
- ☐
- ☐

SOCIAL MEDIA

- ☐ ✉
- ☐ Instagram
- ☐ Facebook
- ☐ Twitter
- ☐ Pinterest
- ☐ WordPress

LINKS

YouTube *Planner*

VIDEO TITLE

CATEGORY

DURATION

KEYWORDS

DESCRIPTION

SUPPLIES

CHECKLIST

- ☐ FILM
- ☐ VOICEOVER
- ☐ EDIT
- ☐ THUMBNAIL
- ☐ DESCRIPTION
- ☐ TAG
- ☐ UPLOAD
- ☐ EFFECTS
- ☐ MUSIC
- ☐ POSTED

TALK ABOUT

SOCIAL MEDIA

- ☐ ✉
- ☐ Instagram
- ☐ Facebook
- ☐ Twitter
- ☐ Pinterest
- ☐ WordPress

LINKS

YouTube *Planner*

VIDEO TITLE

CATEGORY

DURATION

KEYWORDS

DESCRIPTION

SUPPLIES

CHECKLIST

- ☐ FILM
- ☐ VOICEOVER
- ☐ EDIT
- ☐ THUMBNAIL
- ☐ DESCRIPTION
- ☐ TAG
- ☐ UPLOAD
- ☐ EFFECTS
- ☐ MUSIC
- ☐ POSTED

TALK ABOUT

- ☐
- ☐
- ☐
- ☐
- ☐
- ☐
- ☐
- ☐
- ☐
- ☐
- ☐
- ☐

SOCIAL MEDIA

- ☐ ✉
- ☐ Instagram
- ☐ Facebook
- ☐ Twitter
- ☐ Pinterest
- ☐ WordPress

LINKS

YouTube *Planner*

VIDEO TITLE	CATEGORY	DURATION
KEYWORDS		

DESCRIPTION

SUPPLIES

CHECKLIST

- ☐ FILM
- ☐ VOICEOVER
- ☐ EDIT
- ☐ THUMBNAIL
- ☐ DESCRIPTION
- ☐ TAG
- ☐ UPLOAD
- ☐ EFFECTS
- ☐ MUSIC
- ☐ POSTED

TALK ABOUT

- ☐
- ☐
- ☐
- ☐
- ☐
- ☐
- ☐
- ☐
- ☐
- ☐

SOCIAL MEDIA

- ☐ ✉
- ☐ Instagram
- ☐ Facebook
- ☐ Twitter
- ☐ Pinterest
- ☐ WordPress

LINKS

YouTube *Planner*

VIDEO TITLE

CATEGORY

DURATION

KEYWORDS

DESCRIPTION

SUPPLIES

CHECKLIST

- ☐ FILM
- ☐ VOICEOVER
- ☐ EDIT
- ☐ THUMBNAIL
- ☐ DESCRIPTION
- ☐ TAG
- ☐ UPLOAD
- ☐ EFFECTS
- ☐ MUSIC
- ☐ POSTED

TALK ABOUT

SOCIAL MEDIA

LINKS

YouTube *Planner*

VIDEO TITLE

CATEGORY

DURATION

KEYWORDS

DESCRIPTION

SUPPLIES

CHECKLIST

- ☐ FILM
- ☐ VOICEOVER
- ☐ EDIT
- ☐ THUMBNAIL
- ☐ DESCRIPTION
- ☐ TAG
- ☐ UPLOAD
- ☐ EFFECTS
- ☐ MUSIC
- ☐ POSTED

TALK ABOUT

- ☐
- ☐
- ☐
- ☐
- ☐
- ☐
- ☐
- ☐
- ☐
- ☐

SOCIAL MEDIA

- ☐ ✉
- ☐ Instagram
- ☐ Facebook
- ☐ Twitter
- ☐ Pinterest
- ☐ WordPress

LINKS

YouTube *Planner*

| VIDEO TITLE | CATEGORY | DURATION |

KEYWORDS

DESCRIPTION

SUPPLIES

CHECKLIST

- [ ] 🎥 FILM
- [ ] 🎤 VOICEOVER
- [ ] 📝 EDIT
- [ ] 🖼 THUMBNAIL
- [ ] 📄 DESCRIPTION
- [ ] 🏷 TAG
- [ ] 📤 UPLOAD
- [ ] ✨ EFFECTS
- [ ] 🎵 MUSIC
- [ ] 🎉 POSTED

TALK ABOUT

- [ ]
- [ ]
- [ ]
- [ ]
- [ ]
- [ ]
- [ ]
- [ ]
- [ ]
- [ ]
- [ ]
- [ ]

SOCIAL MEDIA

- [ ] ✉️
- [ ] 📷 Instagram
- [ ] f Facebook
- [ ] 🐦 Twitter
- [ ] P Pinterest
- [ ] W WordPress

LINKS

YouTube *Planner*

| VIDEO TITLE | CATEGORY | DURATION |

KEYWORDS

DESCRIPTION

SUPPLIES

CHECKLIST

TALK ABOUT

- ☐ 🎥 FILM
- ☐ 🎤 VOICEOVER
- ☐ 📝 EDIT
- ☐ 🖼 THUMBNAIL
- ☐ 📄 DESCRIPTION
- ☐ 🏷 TAG
- ☐ ⬆ UPLOAD
- ☐ ✨ EFFECTS
- ☐ 🎵 MUSIC
- ☐ 🎉 POSTED

SOCIAL MEDIA

☐ ✉ ☐ 📷 ☐ f
☐ 🐦 ☐ P ☐ W

LINKS

YouTube *Planner*

VIDEO TITLE

CATEGORY

DURATION

KEYWORDS

DESCRIPTION

SUPPLIES

CHECKLIST

- ☐ FILM
- ☐ VOICEOVER
- ☐ EDIT
- ☐ THUMBNAIL
- ☐ DESCRIPTION
- ☐ TAG
- ☐ UPLOAD
- ☐ EFFECTS
- ☐ MUSIC
- ☐ POSTED

TALK ABOUT

- ☐
- ☐
- ☐
- ☐
- ☐
- ☐
- ☐
- ☐
- ☐
- ☐
- ☐
- ☐

SOCIAL MEDIA

- ☐ ✉
- ☐ Instagram
- ☐ Facebook
- ☐ Twitter
- ☐ Pinterest
- ☐ WordPress

LINKS

YouTube *Planner*

VIDEO TITLE

CATEGORY

DURATION

KEYWORDS

DESCRIPTION

SUPPLIES

CHECKLIST

- ☐ FILM
- ☐ VOICEOVER
- ☐ EDIT
- ☐ THUMBNAIL
- ☐ DESCRIPTION
- ☐ TAG
- ☐ UPLOAD
- ☐ EFFECTS
- ☐ MUSIC
- ☐ POSTED

TALK ABOUT

- ☐
- ☐
- ☐
- ☐
- ☐
- ☐
- ☐
- ☐
- ☐
- ☐
- ☐

SOCIAL MEDIA

- ☐ ✉
- ☐ Instagram
- ☐ Facebook
- ☐ Twitter
- ☐ Pinterest
- ☐ WordPress

LINKS

YouTube *Planner*

VIDEO TITLE	CATEGORY	DURATION
KEYWORDS	📅	🕐

DESCRIPTION

SUPPLIES

CHECKLIST

- ☐ 🎥 FILM
- ☐ 🎤 VOICEOVER
- ☐ 📝 EDIT
- ☐ 🖼 THUMBNAIL
- ☐ 📄 DESCRIPTION
- ☐ 🏷 TAG
- ☐ ⬆ UPLOAD
- ☐ ✨ EFFECTS
- ☐ 🎵 MUSIC
- ☐ 🎉 POSTED

TALK ABOUT

☐
☐
☐
☐
☐
☐
☐
☐
☐
☐
☐
☐

SOCIAL MEDIA

- ☐ ✉
- ☐ 📷
- ☐ f
- ☐ 🐦
- ☐ Ⓟ
- ☐ Ⓦ

LINKS

YouTube *Planner*

| VIDEO TITLE | CATEGORY | DURATION |

KEYWORDS

DESCRIPTION

SUPPLIES

CHECKLIST

- ☐ FILM
- ☐ VOICEOVER
- ☐ EDIT
- ☐ THUMBNAIL
- ☐ DESCRIPTION
- ☐ TAG
- ☐ UPLOAD
- ☐ EFFECTS
- ☐ MUSIC
- ☐ POSTED

TALK ABOUT

SOCIAL MEDIA

- ☐ ✉
- ☐ Instagram
- ☐ Facebook
- ☐ Twitter
- ☐ Pinterest
- ☐ WordPress

LINKS

YouTube *Planner*

| VIDEO TITLE | CATEGORY | DURATION |
| KEYWORDS | 📅 | 🕐 |

DESCRIPTION

SUPPLIES

CHECKLIST

- ☐ 🎥 FILM
- ☐ 🎤 VOICEOVER
- ☐ 📝 EDIT
- ☐ 🖼 THUMBNAIL
- ☐ 📄 DESCRIPTION
- ☐ 🏷 TAG
- ☐ ⬆ UPLOAD
- ☐ ✨ EFFECTS
- ☐ 🎵 MUSIC
- ☐ 🎉 POSTED

TALK ABOUT

- ☐
- ☐
- ☐
- ☐
- ☐
- ☐
- ☐
- ☐
- ☐
- ☐
- ☐
- ☐

SOCIAL MEDIA

- ☐ ✉
- ☐ Instagram
- ☐ Facebook
- ☐ Twitter
- ☐ Pinterest
- ☐ WordPress

LINKS

YouTube *Planner*

VIDEO TITLE	CATEGORY	DURATION
KEYWORDS	📅	🕐

DESCRIPTION

SUPPLIES

CHECKLIST

- ☐ 🎥 FILM
- ☐ 🎤 VOICEOVER
- ☐ 📝 EDIT
- ☐ 🖼 THUMBNAIL
- ☐ 📄 DESCRIPTION
- ☐ 🏷 TAG
- ☐ ⬆ UPLOAD
- ☐ ✨ EFFECTS
- ☐ 🎵 MUSIC
- ☐ 🎉 POSTED

TALK ABOUT

- ☐
- ☐
- ☐
- ☐
- ☐
- ☐
- ☐
- ☐
- ☐
- ☐
- ☐
- ☐

SOCIAL MEDIA

- ☐ ✉
- ☐ 📷 Instagram
- ☐ f Facebook
- ☐ 🐦 Twitter
- ☐ 📌 Pinterest
- ☐ Ⓦ WordPress

LINKS

YouTube *Planner*

VIDEO TITLE

CATEGORY

DURATION

KEYWORDS

DESCRIPTION

SUPPLIES

CHECKLIST

- ☐ FILM
- ☐ VOICEOVER
- ☐ EDIT
- ☐ THUMBNAIL
- ☐ DESCRIPTION
- ☐ TAG
- ☐ UPLOAD
- ☐ EFFECTS
- ☐ MUSIC
- ☐ POSTED

TALK ABOUT

☐
☐
☐
☐
☐
☐
☐
☐
☐
☐
☐
☐

SOCIAL MEDIA

- ☐ ✉
- ☐ Instagram
- ☐ Facebook
- ☐ Twitter
- ☐ Pinterest
- ☐ WordPress

LINKS

YouTube *Planner*

VIDEO TITLE

CATEGORY

DURATION

KEYWORDS

DESCRIPTION

SUPPLIES

CHECKLIST

- ☐ FILM
- ☐ VOICEOVER
- ☐ EDIT
- ☐ THUMBNAIL
- ☐ DESCRIPTION
- ☐ TAG
- ☐ UPLOAD
- ☐ EFFECTS
- ☐ MUSIC
- ☐ POSTED

TALK ABOUT

SOCIAL MEDIA

- ☐ ✉
- ☐ Instagram
- ☐ Facebook
- ☐ Twitter
- ☐ Pinterest
- ☐ WordPress

LINKS

YouTube *Planner*

VIDEO TITLE

CATEGORY

DURATION

KEYWORDS

DESCRIPTION

SUPPLIES

CHECKLIST

- ☐ FILM
- ☐ VOICEOVER
- ☐ EDIT
- ☐ THUMBNAIL
- ☐ DESCRIPTION
- ☐ TAG
- ☐ UPLOAD
- ☐ EFFECTS
- ☐ MUSIC
- ☐ POSTED

TALK ABOUT

SOCIAL MEDIA

- ☐ ✉
- ☐ Instagram
- ☐ Facebook
- ☐ Twitter
- ☐ Pinterest
- ☐ WordPress

LINKS

YouTube *Planner*

VIDEO TITLE	CATEGORY	DURATION
KEYWORDS		

DESCRIPTION

SUPPLIES

CHECKLIST

- ☐ FILM
- ☐ VOICEOVER
- ☐ EDIT
- ☐ THUMBNAIL
- ☐ DESCRIPTION
- ☐ TAG
- ☐ UPLOAD
- ☐ EFFECTS
- ☐ MUSIC
- ☐ POSTED

TALK ABOUT

- ☐
- ☐
- ☐
- ☐
- ☐
- ☐
- ☐
- ☐
- ☐
- ☐
- ☐

SOCIAL MEDIA

- ☐ ✉
- ☐ Instagram
- ☐ Facebook
- ☐ Twitter
- ☐ Pinterest
- ☐ WordPress

LINKS

YouTube *Planner*

VIDEO TITLE

CATEGORY

DURATION

KEYWORDS

DESCRIPTION

SUPPLIES

CHECKLIST

TALK ABOUT

- ☐ 🎥 FILM
- ☐ 🎤 VOICEOVER
- ☐ 📝 EDIT
- ☐ 🖼 THUMBNAIL
- ☐ 📄 DESCRIPTION
- ☐ 🏷 TAG
- ☐ ⬆ UPLOAD
- ☐ ✨ EFFECTS
- ☐ 🎵 MUSIC
- ☐ 🎉 POSTED

SOCIAL MEDIA

- ☐ ✉
- ☐ 📷
- ☐ f
- ☐ 🐦
- ☐ P
- ☐ W

LINKS

YouTube *Planner*

VIDEO TITLE | **CATEGORY** | **DURATION**

KEYWORDS

DESCRIPTION

SUPPLIES

CHECKLIST

- ☐ FILM
- ☐ VOICEOVER
- ☐ EDIT
- ☐ THUMBNAIL
- ☐ DESCRIPTION
- ☐ TAG
- ☐ UPLOAD
- ☐ EFFECTS
- ☐ MUSIC
- ☐ POSTED

TALK ABOUT

SOCIAL MEDIA

- ☐ ✉
- ☐ 📷
- ☐ f
- ☐ 🐦
- ☐ P
- ☐ W

LINKS

YouTube *Planner*

VIDEO TITLE	CATEGORY	DURATION

KEYWORDS		

DESCRIPTION

SUPPLIES

CHECKLIST

- ☐ 🎥 FILM
- ☐ 🎤 VOICEOVER
- ☐ 📝 EDIT
- ☐ 🖼 THUMBNAIL
- ☐ 📄 DESCRIPTION
- ☐ 🏷 TAG
- ☐ ⬆ UPLOAD
- ☐ ✨ EFFECTS
- ☐ 🎵 MUSIC
- ☐ 🎉 POSTED

TALK ABOUT

- ☐
- ☐
- ☐
- ☐
- ☐
- ☐
- ☐
- ☐
- ☐
- ☐
- ☐

SOCIAL MEDIA

- ☐ ✉
- ☐ 🐦
- ☐ 📷
- ☐ P
- ☐ f
- ☐ W

LINKS

YouTube *Planner*

VIDEO TITLE

CATEGORY

DURATION

KEYWORDS

DESCRIPTION

SUPPLIES

CHECKLIST

- ☐ FILM
- ☐ VOICEOVER
- ☐ EDIT
- ☐ THUMBNAIL
- ☐ DESCRIPTION
- ☐ TAG
- ☐ UPLOAD
- ☐ EFFECTS
- ☐ MUSIC
- ☐ POSTED

TALK ABOUT

☐
☐
☐
☐
☐
☐
☐
☐
☐
☐
☐

SOCIAL MEDIA

- ☐ ✉
- ☐ Instagram
- ☐ Facebook
- ☐ Twitter
- ☐ Pinterest
- ☐ WordPress

LINKS

YouTube *Planner*

VIDEO TITLE

CATEGORY

DURATION

KEYWORDS

DESCRIPTION

SUPPLIES

CHECKLIST

- ☐ FILM
- ☐ VOICEOVER
- ☐ EDIT
- ☐ THUMBNAIL
- ☐ DESCRIPTION
- ☐ TAG
- ☐ UPLOAD
- ☐ EFFECTS
- ☐ MUSIC
- ☐ POSTED

TALK ABOUT

- ☐
- ☐
- ☐
- ☐
- ☐
- ☐
- ☐
- ☐
- ☐
- ☐

SOCIAL MEDIA

- ☐ ✉
- ☐ Instagram
- ☐ Facebook
- ☐ Twitter
- ☐ Pinterest
- ☐ WordPress

LINKS

YouTube *Planner*

VIDEO TITLE

CATEGORY

DURATION

KEYWORDS

DESCRIPTION

SUPPLIES

CHECKLIST

- ☐ FILM
- ☐ VOICEOVER
- ☐ EDIT
- ☐ THUMBNAIL
- ☐ DESCRIPTION
- ☐ TAG
- ☐ UPLOAD
- ☐ EFFECTS
- ☐ MUSIC
- ☐ POSTED

TALK ABOUT

SOCIAL MEDIA

- ☐ ✉
- ☐ Instagram
- ☐ Facebook
- ☐ Twitter
- ☐ Pinterest
- ☐ WordPress

LINKS

YouTube *Planner*

VIDEO TITLE

CATEGORY

DURATION

KEYWORDS

DESCRIPTION

SUPPLIES

CHECKLIST

TALK ABOUT

- [ ] 🎥 FILM
- [ ] 🎤 VOICEOVER
- [ ] 📝 EDIT
- [ ] 🖼 THUMBNAIL
- [ ] 📄 DESCRIPTION
- [ ] 🏷 TAG
- [ ] ⬆ UPLOAD
- [ ] ✨ EFFECTS
- [ ] 🎵 MUSIC
- [ ] 🎉 POSTED

SOCIAL MEDIA

- [ ] ✉
- [ ] 📷
- [ ] f
- [ ] 🐦
- [ ] P
- [ ] W

LINKS

YouTube *Planner*

| VIDEO TITLE | CATEGORY | DURATION |

KEYWORDS

DESCRIPTION

SUPPLIES

CHECKLIST

- [ ] 🎥 FILM
- [ ] 🎤 VOICEOVER
- [ ] 📝 EDIT
- [ ] 🖼 THUMBNAIL
- [ ] 📄 DESCRIPTION
- [ ] 🏷 TAG
- [ ] ⬆ UPLOAD
- [ ] ✨ EFFECTS
- [ ] 🎵 MUSIC
- [ ] 🎉 POSTED

TALK ABOUT

- [ ]
- [ ]
- [ ]
- [ ]
- [ ]
- [ ]
- [ ]
- [ ]
- [ ]
- [ ]
- [ ]
- [ ]

SOCIAL MEDIA

- [ ] ✉ Email
- [ ] 📷 Instagram
- [ ] f Facebook
- [ ] 🐦 Twitter
- [ ] 📌 Pinterest
- [ ] W WordPress

LINKS

YouTube *Planner*

VIDEO TITLE

CATEGORY

DURATION

KEYWORDS

DESCRIPTION

SUPPLIES

CHECKLIST

- [ ] 🎥 FILM
- [ ] 🎤 VOICEOVER
- [ ] 📝 EDIT
- [ ] 🖼 THUMBNAIL
- [ ] 📄 DESCRIPTION
- [ ] 🏷 TAG
- [ ] ⬆ UPLOAD
- [ ] ✨ EFFECTS
- [ ] 🎵 MUSIC
- [ ] 🎉 POSTED

TALK ABOUT

- [ ]
- [ ]
- [ ]
- [ ]
- [ ]
- [ ]
- [ ]
- [ ]
- [ ]
- [ ]
- [ ]
- [ ]

SOCIAL MEDIA

- [ ] ✉
- [ ] 📷
- [ ] f
- [ ] 🐦
- [ ] P
- [ ] W

LINKS

YouTube *Planner*

| VIDEO TITLE | CATEGORY | DURATION |

KEYWORDS

DESCRIPTION

SUPPLIES

CHECKLIST

- ☐ FILM
- ☐ VOICEOVER
- ☐ EDIT
- ☐ THUMBNAIL
- ☐ DESCRIPTION
- ☐ TAG
- ☐ UPLOAD
- ☐ EFFECTS
- ☐ MUSIC
- ☐ POSTED

TALK ABOUT

SOCIAL MEDIA

- ☐ ✉
- ☐ Instagram
- ☐ Facebook
- ☐ Twitter
- ☐ Pinterest
- ☐ WordPress

LINKS

YouTube *Planner*

VIDEO TITLE

CATEGORY

DURATION

KEYWORDS

DESCRIPTION

SUPPLIES

CHECKLIST

- [ ] FILM
- [ ] VOICEOVER
- [ ] EDIT
- [ ] THUMBNAIL
- [ ] DESCRIPTION
- [ ] TAG
- [ ] UPLOAD
- [ ] EFFECTS
- [ ] MUSIC
- [ ] POSTED

TALK ABOUT

SOCIAL MEDIA

- [ ] ✉
- [ ] Instagram
- [ ] Facebook
- [ ] Twitter
- [ ] Pinterest
- [ ] WordPress

LINKS

YouTube *Planner*

VIDEO TITLE	CATEGORY	DURATION

KEYWORDS

DESCRIPTION

SUPPLIES

CHECKLIST

- ☐ 🎥 FILM
- ☐ 🎤 VOICEOVER
- ☐ 📝 EDIT
- ☐ 🖼 THUMBNAIL
- ☐ 📄 DESCRIPTION
- ☐ 🏷 TAG
- ☐ ⬆ UPLOAD
- ☐ ✨ EFFECTS
- ☐ 🎵 MUSIC
- ☐ 🎉 POSTED

TALK ABOUT

- ☐
- ☐
- ☐
- ☐
- ☐
- ☐
- ☐
- ☐
- ☐
- ☐
- ☐
- ☐

SOCIAL MEDIA

- ☐ ✉
- ☐ 🐦
- ☐ 📷
- ☐ 📌
- ☐ f
- ☐ W

LINKS

YouTube *Planner*

| VIDEO TITLE | CATEGORY | DURATION |
| KEYWORDS | 📅 | 🕒 |

DESCRIPTION

SUPPLIES

CHECKLIST

- ☐ 🎥 FILM
- ☐ 🎤 VOICEOVER
- ☐ 📝 EDIT
- ☐ 🖼 THUMBNAIL
- ☐ 📄 DESCRIPTION
- ☐ 🏷 TAG
- ☐ ⬆ UPLOAD
- ☐ ✨ EFFECTS
- ☐ 🎵 MUSIC
- ☐ 🎉 POSTED

TALK ABOUT

☐
☐
☐
☐
☐
☐
☐
☐
☐
☐
☐

SOCIAL MEDIA

- ☐ ✉
- ☐ 📷 (Instagram)
- ☐ f (Facebook)
- ☐ 🐦 (Twitter)
- ☐ 📌 (Pinterest)
- ☐ Ⓦ (WordPress)

LINKS

YouTube *Planner*

VIDEO TITLE	CATEGORY	DURATION
KEYWORDS		

DESCRIPTION

SUPPLIES

CHECKLIST

- ☐ FILM
- ☐ VOICEOVER
- ☐ EDIT
- ☐ THUMBNAIL
- ☐ DESCRIPTION
- ☐ TAG
- ☐ UPLOAD
- ☐ EFFECTS
- ☐ MUSIC
- ☐ POSTED

TALK ABOUT

☐
☐
☐
☐
☐
☐
☐
☐
☐
☐

SOCIAL MEDIA

- ☐ ✉
- ☐ Instagram
- ☐ Facebook
- ☐ Twitter
- ☐ Pinterest
- ☐ WordPress

LINKS

YouTube *Planner*

| VIDEO TITLE | CATEGORY | DURATION |

KEYWORDS

DESCRIPTION

SUPPLIES

CHECKLIST

- [ ] FILM
- [ ] VOICEOVER
- [ ] EDIT
- [ ] THUMBNAIL
- [ ] DESCRIPTION
- [ ] TAG
- [ ] UPLOAD
- [ ] EFFECTS
- [ ] MUSIC
- [ ] POSTED

TALK ABOUT

- [ ]
- [ ]
- [ ]
- [ ]
- [ ]
- [ ]
- [ ]
- [ ]
- [ ]
- [ ]
- [ ]
- [ ]

SOCIAL MEDIA

- [ ] ✉
- [ ] Instagram
- [ ] Facebook
- [ ] Twitter
- [ ] Pinterest
- [ ] WordPress

LINKS

YouTube *Planner*

VIDEO TITLE	CATEGORY	DURATION
KEYWORDS		

DESCRIPTION

SUPPLIES

CHECKLIST

- ☐ FILM
- ☐ VOICEOVER
- ☐ EDIT
- ☐ THUMBNAIL
- ☐ DESCRIPTION
- ☐ TAG
- ☐ UPLOAD
- ☐ EFFECTS
- ☐ MUSIC
- ☐ POSTED

TALK ABOUT

SOCIAL MEDIA

- ☐ Email
- ☐ Instagram
- ☐ Facebook
- ☐ Twitter
- ☐ Pinterest
- ☐ WordPress

LINKS

YouTube *Planner*

VIDEO TITLE	CATEGORY	DURATION
KEYWORDS		

DESCRIPTION

SUPPLIES

CHECKLIST

- [ ] 🎥 FILM
- [ ] 🎤 VOICEOVER
- [ ] 📝 EDIT
- [ ] 🖼 THUMBNAIL
- [ ] 📄 DESCRIPTION
- [ ] 🏷 TAG
- [ ] ⬆ UPLOAD
- [ ] ✨ EFFECTS
- [ ] 🎵 MUSIC
- [ ] 🎉 POSTED

TALK ABOUT

- [ ]
- [ ]
- [ ]
- [ ]
- [ ]
- [ ]
- [ ]
- [ ]
- [ ]
- [ ]
- [ ]
- [ ]

SOCIAL MEDIA

- [ ] ✉ Email
- [ ] 📷 Instagram
- [ ] f Facebook
- [ ] 🐦 Twitter
- [ ] 📌 Pinterest
- [ ] Ⓦ WordPress

LINKS

YouTube *Planner*

VIDEO TITLE

CATEGORY

DURATION

KEYWORDS

DESCRIPTION

SUPPLIES

CHECKLIST

- ☐ FILM
- ☐ VOICEOVER
- ☐ EDIT
- ☐ THUMBNAIL
- ☐ DESCRIPTION
- ☐ TAG
- ☐ UPLOAD
- ☐ EFFECTS
- ☐ MUSIC
- ☐ POSTED

TALK ABOUT

- ☐
- ☐
- ☐
- ☐
- ☐
- ☐
- ☐
- ☐
- ☐
- ☐
- ☐
- ☐

SOCIAL MEDIA

- ☐ ✉
- ☐ Instagram
- ☐ Facebook
- ☐ Twitter
- ☐ Pinterest
- ☐ WordPress

LINKS

YouTube *Planner*

| VIDEO TITLE | CATEGORY | DURATION |

KEYWORDS

DESCRIPTION

SUPPLIES

CHECKLIST

- ☐ FILM
- ☐ VOICEOVER
- ☐ EDIT
- ☐ THUMBNAIL
- ☐ DESCRIPTION
- ☐ TAG
- ☐ UPLOAD
- ☐ EFFECTS
- ☐ MUSIC
- ☐ POSTED

TALK ABOUT

SOCIAL MEDIA

LINKS

YouTube *Planner*

VIDEO TITLE	CATEGORY	DURATION
KEYWORDS	📅	🕐

DESCRIPTION

SUPPLIES

CHECKLIST

- ☐ 🎥 FILM
- ☐ 🎤 VOICEOVER
- ☐ 📝 EDIT
- ☐ 🖼 THUMBNAIL
- ☐ 📄 DESCRIPTION
- ☐ 🏷 TAG
- ☐ ⬆ UPLOAD
- ☐ ✨ EFFECTS
- ☐ 🎵 MUSIC
- ☐ 🎉 POSTED

TALK ABOUT

SOCIAL MEDIA

- ☐ ✉
- ☐ 📷
- ☐ f
- ☐ 🐦
- ☐ P
- ☐ W

LINKS

YouTube *Planner*

VIDEO TITLE

CATEGORY

DURATION

KEYWORDS

DESCRIPTION

SUPPLIES

CHECKLIST

- ☐ 🎥 FILM
- ☐ 🎤 VOICEOVER
- ☐ 📝 EDIT
- ☐ 🖼 THUMBNAIL
- ☐ 📄 DESCRIPTION
- ☐ 🏷 TAG
- ☐ ⬆ UPLOAD
- ☐ ✨ EFFECTS
- ☐ 🎵 MUSIC
- ☐ 🎉 POSTED

TALK ABOUT

☐ _____
☐ _____
☐ _____
☐ _____
☐ _____
☐ _____
☐ _____
☐ _____
☐ _____
☐ _____

SOCIAL MEDIA

☐ ✉   ☐ 📷   ☐ f
☐ 🐦   ☐ ⓟ   ☐ Ⓦ

LINKS

YouTube *Planner*

VIDEO TITLE	CATEGORY	DURATION
KEYWORDS	📅	🕐

DESCRIPTION

SUPPLIES

CHECKLIST

- ☐ 🎥 FILM
- ☐ 🎤 VOICEOVER
- ☐ 📝 EDIT
- ☐ 🖼 THUMBNAIL
- ☐ 📄 DESCRIPTION
- ☐ 🏷 TAG
- ☐ ⬆ UPLOAD
- ☐ ✨ EFFECTS
- ☐ 🎵 MUSIC
- ☐ 🎉 POSTED

TALK ABOUT

☐
☐
☐
☐
☐
☐
☐
☐
☐
☐
☐

SOCIAL MEDIA

- ☐ ✉
- ☐ 📷
- ☐ f
- ☐ 🐦
- ☐ 📌
- ☐ W

LINKS

YouTube *Planner*

VIDEO TITLE	CATEGORY	DURATION
KEYWORDS	📅	🕐

DESCRIPTION

SUPPLIES

CHECKLIST

- ☐ 🎥 FILM
- ☐ 🎤 VOICEOVER
- ☐ 📝 EDIT
- ☐ 🖼 THUMBNAIL
- ☐ 📄 DESCRIPTION
- ☐ 🏷 TAG
- ☐ ⬆ UPLOAD
- ☐ ✨ EFFECTS
- ☐ 🎵 MUSIC
- ☐ 🎉 POSTED

TALK ABOUT

- ☐
- ☐
- ☐
- ☐
- ☐
- ☐
- ☐
- ☐
- ☐
- ☐
- ☐
- ☐

SOCIAL MEDIA

- ☐ ✉
- ☐ 📷 Instagram
- ☐ f Facebook
- ☐ 🐦 Twitter
- ☐ 📌 Pinterest
- ☐ Ⓦ WordPress

LINKS

YouTube *Planner*

VIDEO TITLE	CATEGORY	DURATION
KEYWORDS		

DESCRIPTION

SUPPLIES

CHECKLIST

- ☐ FILM
- ☐ VOICEOVER
- ☐ EDIT
- ☐ THUMBNAIL
- ☐ DESCRIPTION
- ☐ TAG
- ☐ UPLOAD
- ☐ EFFECTS
- ☐ MUSIC
- ☐ POSTED

TALK ABOUT

- ☐
- ☐
- ☐
- ☐
- ☐
- ☐
- ☐
- ☐
- ☐
- ☐

SOCIAL MEDIA

- ☐ ✉
- ☐ Instagram
- ☐ Facebook
- ☐ Twitter
- ☐ Pinterest
- ☐ WordPress

LINKS

YouTube *Planner*

VIDEO TITLE	CATEGORY	DURATION
KEYWORDS		

DESCRIPTION

SUPPLIES

CHECKLIST

- ☐ 🎥 FILM
- ☐ 🎤 VOICEOVER
- ☐ 📝 EDIT
- ☐ 🖼 THUMBNAIL
- ☐ 📄 DESCRIPTION
- ☐ 🏷 TAG
- ☐ ⬆ UPLOAD
- ☐ ✨ EFFECTS
- ☐ 🎵 MUSIC
- ☐ 🎉 POSTED

TALK ABOUT

☐
☐
☐
☐
☐
☐
☐
☐
☐
☐
☐
☐

SOCIAL MEDIA

- ☐ ✉
- ☐ 📷
- ☐ f
- ☐ 🐦
- ☐ ℗
- ☐ Ⓦ

LINKS

YouTube *Planner*

VIDEO TITLE	CATEGORY	DURATION
KEYWORDS		

DESCRIPTION

SUPPLIES

CHECKLIST

- ☐ FILM
- ☐ VOICEOVER
- ☐ EDIT
- ☐ THUMBNAIL
- ☐ DESCRIPTION
- ☐ TAG
- ☐ UPLOAD
- ☐ EFFECTS
- ☐ MUSIC
- ☐ POSTED

TALK ABOUT

- ☐
- ☐
- ☐
- ☐
- ☐
- ☐
- ☐
- ☐
- ☐
- ☐
- ☐

SOCIAL MEDIA

- ☐ ✉
- ☐ Instagram
- ☐ Facebook
- ☐ Twitter
- ☐ Pinterest
- ☐ WordPress

LINKS

YouTube *Planner*

VIDEO TITLE

CATEGORY

DURATION

KEYWORDS

DESCRIPTION

SUPPLIES

CHECKLIST

- [ ] FILM
- [ ] VOICEOVER
- [ ] EDIT
- [ ] THUMBNAIL
- [ ] DESCRIPTION
- [ ] TAG
- [ ] UPLOAD
- [ ] EFFECTS
- [ ] MUSIC
- [ ] POSTED

TALK ABOUT

SOCIAL MEDIA

LINKS

YouTube *Planner*

| VIDEO TITLE | CATEGORY | DURATION |
| KEYWORDS | 📅 | 🕐 |

DESCRIPTION

SUPPLIES

CHECKLIST

- ☐ 🎥 FILM
- ☐ 🎤 VOICEOVER
- ☐ 📝 EDIT
- ☐ 🖼 THUMBNAIL
- ☐ 📄 DESCRIPTION
- ☐ 🏷 TAG
- ☐ ⬆ UPLOAD
- ☐ ✨ EFFECTS
- ☐ 🎵 MUSIC
- ☐ 🎉 POSTED

TALK ABOUT

- ☐
- ☐
- ☐
- ☐
- ☐
- ☐
- ☐
- ☐
- ☐
- ☐
- ☐

SOCIAL MEDIA

- ☐ ✉
- ☐ 📷 Instagram
- ☐ f Facebook
- ☐ 🐦 Twitter
- ☐ P Pinterest
- ☐ W WordPress

LINKS

YouTube *Planner*

VIDEO TITLE

CATEGORY

DURATION

KEYWORDS

DESCRIPTION

SUPPLIES

CHECKLIST

- ☐ 🎥 FILM
- ☐ 🎤 VOICEOVER
- ☐ 📝 EDIT
- ☐ 🖼 THUMBNAIL
- ☐ 📄 DESCRIPTION
- ☐ 🏷 TAG
- ☐ ⬆ UPLOAD
- ☐ ✨ EFFECTS
- ☐ 🎵 MUSIC
- ☐ 🎉 POSTED

TALK ABOUT

- ☐
- ☐
- ☐
- ☐
- ☐
- ☐
- ☐
- ☐
- ☐
- ☐
- ☐
- ☐

SOCIAL MEDIA

- ☐ ✉
- ☐ 📷
- ☐ f
- ☐ 🐦
- ☐ Ⓟ
- ☐ W

LINKS

YouTube *Planner*

| VIDEO TITLE | CATEGORY | DURATION |

KEYWORDS

DESCRIPTION

SUPPLIES

CHECKLIST

- ☐ FILM
- ☐ VOICEOVER
- ☐ EDIT
- ☐ THUMBNAIL
- ☐ DESCRIPTION
- ☐ TAG
- ☐ UPLOAD
- ☐ EFFECTS
- ☐ MUSIC
- ☐ POSTED

TALK ABOUT

SOCIAL MEDIA

LINKS

YouTube *Planner*

VIDEO TITLE	CATEGORY	DURATION
KEYWORDS	📅	🕐

DESCRIPTION

SUPPLIES

CHECKLIST

- ☐ 🎥 FILM
- ☐ 🎤 VOICEOVER
- ☐ 📝 EDIT
- ☐ 🖼 THUMBNAIL
- ☐ 📄 DESCRIPTION
- ☐ 🏷 TAG
- ☐ ⬆ UPLOAD
- ☐ ✨ EFFECTS
- ☐ 🎵 MUSIC
- ☐ 🎉 POSTED

TALK ABOUT

- ☐
- ☐
- ☐
- ☐
- ☐
- ☐
- ☐
- ☐
- ☐
- ☐
- ☐

SOCIAL MEDIA

- ☐ ✉
- ☐ 📷 Instagram
- ☐ f Facebook
- ☐ 🐦 Twitter
- ☐ 📌 Pinterest
- ☐ Ⓦ WordPress

LINKS

YouTube *Planner*

VIDEO TITLE

CATEGORY

DURATION

KEYWORDS

DESCRIPTION

SUPPLIES

CHECKLIST

- ☐ FILM
- ☐ VOICEOVER
- ☐ EDIT
- ☐ THUMBNAIL
- ☐ DESCRIPTION
- ☐ TAG
- ☐ UPLOAD
- ☐ EFFECTS
- ☐ MUSIC
- ☐ POSTED

TALK ABOUT

SOCIAL MEDIA

LINKS

YouTube *Planner*

| VIDEO TITLE | CATEGORY | DURATION |

KEYWORDS

DESCRIPTION

SUPPLIES

CHECKLIST

- ☐ FILM
- ☐ VOICEOVER
- ☐ EDIT
- ☐ THUMBNAIL
- ☐ DESCRIPTION
- ☐ TAG
- ☐ UPLOAD
- ☐ EFFECTS
- ☐ MUSIC
- ☐ POSTED

TALK ABOUT

SOCIAL MEDIA

LINKS

YouTube *Planner*

VIDEO TITLE	CATEGORY	DURATION
KEYWORDS		

DESCRIPTION

SUPPLIES

CHECKLIST

- ☐ FILM
- ☐ VOICEOVER
- ☐ EDIT
- ☐ THUMBNAIL
- ☐ DESCRIPTION
- ☐ TAG
- ☐ UPLOAD
- ☐ EFFECTS
- ☐ MUSIC
- ☐ POSTED

TALK ABOUT

☐
☐
☐
☐
☐
☐
☐
☐
☐
☐
☐

SOCIAL MEDIA

☐ ✉ ☐ 📷 ☐ f
☐ 🐦 ☐ P ☐ W

LINKS

YouTube *Planner*

VIDEO TITLE

CATEGORY

DURATION

KEYWORDS

DESCRIPTION

SUPPLIES

CHECKLIST

- ☐ FILM
- ☐ VOICEOVER
- ☐ EDIT
- ☐ THUMBNAIL
- ☐ DESCRIPTION
- ☐ TAG
- ☐ UPLOAD
- ☐ EFFECTS
- ☐ MUSIC
- ☐ POSTED

TALK ABOUT

SOCIAL MEDIA

- ☐ ✉
- ☐ Instagram
- ☐ Facebook
- ☐ Twitter
- ☐ Pinterest
- ☐ WordPress

LINKS

YouTube *Planner*

| VIDEO TITLE | CATEGORY | DURATION |

KEYWORDS

DESCRIPTION

SUPPLIES

CHECKLIST

- ☐ 🎥 FILM
- ☐ 🎤 VOICEOVER
- ☐ 📝 EDIT
- ☐ 🖼 THUMBNAIL
- ☐ 📄 DESCRIPTION
- ☐ 🏷 TAG
- ☐ ⬆ UPLOAD
- ☐ ✨ EFFECTS
- ☐ 🎵 MUSIC
- ☐ 🎉 POSTED

TALK ABOUT

SOCIAL MEDIA

- ☐ ✉
- ☐ 📷
- ☐ f
- ☐ 🐦
- ☐ P
- ☐ Ⓦ

LINKS

YouTube *Planner*

| VIDEO TITLE | CATEGORY | DURATION |

KEYWORDS

DESCRIPTION

SUPPLIES

CHECKLIST

- [ ] FILM
- [ ] VOICEOVER
- [ ] EDIT
- [ ] THUMBNAIL
- [ ] DESCRIPTION
- [ ] TAG
- [ ] UPLOAD
- [ ] EFFECTS
- [ ] MUSIC
- [ ] POSTED

TALK ABOUT

- [ ]
- [ ]
- [ ]
- [ ]
- [ ]
- [ ]
- [ ]
- [ ]
- [ ]
- [ ]
- [ ]
- [ ]

SOCIAL MEDIA

- [ ] ✉
- [ ] Twitter
- [ ] Instagram
- [ ] Pinterest
- [ ] Facebook
- [ ] WordPress

LINKS

YouTube *Planner*

VIDEO TITLE

CATEGORY

DURATION

KEYWORDS

DESCRIPTION

SUPPLIES

CHECKLIST

- ☐ FILM
- ☐ VOICEOVER
- ☐ EDIT
- ☐ THUMBNAIL
- ☐ DESCRIPTION
- ☐ TAG
- ☐ UPLOAD
- ☐ EFFECTS
- ☐ MUSIC
- ☐ POSTED

TALK ABOUT

- ☐
- ☐
- ☐
- ☐
- ☐
- ☐
- ☐
- ☐
- ☐
- ☐
- ☐
- ☐

SOCIAL MEDIA

- ☐ ✉
- ☐ Instagram
- ☐ Facebook
- ☐ Twitter
- ☐ Pinterest
- ☐ WordPress

LINKS

YouTube *Planner*

VIDEO TITLE

CATEGORY

DURATION

KEYWORDS

DESCRIPTION

SUPPLIES

CHECKLIST

- ☐ FILM
- ☐ VOICEOVER
- ☐ EDIT
- ☐ THUMBNAIL
- ☐ DESCRIPTION
- ☐ TAG
- ☐ UPLOAD
- ☐ EFFECTS
- ☐ MUSIC
- ☐ POSTED

TALK ABOUT

- ☐
- ☐
- ☐
- ☐
- ☐
- ☐
- ☐
- ☐
- ☐
- ☐
- ☐

SOCIAL MEDIA

- ☐ ✉
- ☐ Instagram
- ☐ Facebook
- ☐ Twitter
- ☐ Pinterest
- ☐ WordPress

LINKS

YouTube *Planner*

VIDEO TITLE	CATEGORY	DURATION
KEYWORDS		

DESCRIPTION

SUPPLIES

CHECKLIST

- ☐ 🎥 FILM
- ☐ 🎤 VOICEOVER
- ☐ 📝 EDIT
- ☐ 🖼 THUMBNAIL
- ☐ 📄 DESCRIPTION
- ☐ 🏷 TAG
- ☐ ⬆ UPLOAD
- ☐ ✨ EFFECTS
- ☐ 🎵 MUSIC
- ☐ 🎉 POSTED

TALK ABOUT

SOCIAL MEDIA

- ☐ ✉
- ☐ 📷
- ☐ f
- ☐ 🐦
- ☐ P
- ☐ W

LINKS

YouTube *Planner*

VIDEO TITLE

CATEGORY

DURATION

KEYWORDS

DESCRIPTION

SUPPLIES

CHECKLIST

- ☐ FILM
- ☐ VOICEOVER
- ☐ EDIT
- ☐ THUMBNAIL
- ☐ DESCRIPTION
- ☐ TAG
- ☐ UPLOAD
- ☐ EFFECTS
- ☐ MUSIC
- ☐ POSTED

TALK ABOUT

- ☐
- ☐
- ☐
- ☐
- ☐
- ☐
- ☐
- ☐
- ☐
- ☐
- ☐

SOCIAL MEDIA

- ☐ ✉
- ☐ Instagram
- ☐ Facebook
- ☐ Twitter
- ☐ Pinterest
- ☐ WordPress

LINKS

YouTube *Planner*

VIDEO TITLE	CATEGORY	DURATION
KEYWORDS		

DESCRIPTION

SUPPLIES

CHECKLIST

- ☐ 🎥 FILM
- ☐ 🎤 VOICEOVER
- ☐ 📝 EDIT
- ☐ 🖼 THUMBNAIL
- ☐ 📄 DESCRIPTION
- ☐ 🏷 TAG
- ☐ ⬆ UPLOAD
- ☐ ✨ EFFECTS
- ☐ 🎵 MUSIC
- ☐ 🎉 POSTED

TALK ABOUT

SOCIAL MEDIA

- ☐ ✉
- ☐ 📷
- ☐ f
- ☐ 🐦
- ☐ P
- ☐ W

LINKS

YouTube *Planner*

| VIDEO TITLE | CATEGORY | DURATION |

KEYWORDS

DESCRIPTION

SUPPLIES

CHECKLIST

- ☐ 🎥 FILM
- ☐ 🎤 VOICEOVER
- ☐ 📝 EDIT
- ☐ 🖼 THUMBNAIL
- ☐ 📄 DESCRIPTION
- ☐ 🏷 TAG
- ☐ ⬆ UPLOAD
- ☐ ✨ EFFECTS
- ☐ 🎵 MUSIC
- ☐ 🎉 POSTED

TALK ABOUT

SOCIAL MEDIA

- ☐ ✉
- ☐ 📷
- ☐ f
- ☐ 🐦
- ☐ P
- ☐ W

LINKS

YouTube *Planner*

| VIDEO TITLE | CATEGORY | DURATION |

KEYWORDS

DESCRIPTION

SUPPLIES

CHECKLIST

TALK ABOUT

- ☐ 🎥 FILM
- ☐ 🎤 VOICEOVER
- ☐ 📝 EDIT
- ☐ 🖼 THUMBNAIL
- ☐ 📄 DESCRIPTION
- ☐ 🏷 TAG
- ☐ ⬆ UPLOAD
- ☐ ✨ EFFECTS
- ☐ 🎵 MUSIC
- ☐ 🎉 POSTED

SOCIAL MEDIA

- ☐ ✉
- ☐ 📷
- ☐ f
- ☐ 🐦
- ☐ P
- ☐ W

LINKS

YouTube *Planner*

VIDEO TITLE

CATEGORY

DURATION

KEYWORDS

DESCRIPTION

SUPPLIES

CHECKLIST

- ☐ FILM
- ☐ VOICEOVER
- ☐ EDIT
- ☐ THUMBNAIL
- ☐ DESCRIPTION
- ☐ TAG
- ☐ UPLOAD
- ☐ EFFECTS
- ☐ MUSIC
- ☐ POSTED

TALK ABOUT

☐
☐
☐
☐
☐
☐
☐
☐
☐
☐

SOCIAL MEDIA

- ☐ ✉
- ☐ Instagram
- ☐ Facebook
- ☐ Twitter
- ☐ Pinterest
- ☐ WordPress

LINKS

YouTube *Planner*

| VIDEO TITLE | CATEGORY | DURATION |

KEYWORDS

DESCRIPTION

SUPPLIES

CHECKLIST

- ☐ FILM
- ☐ VOICEOVER
- ☐ EDIT
- ☐ THUMBNAIL
- ☐ DESCRIPTION
- ☐ TAG
- ☐ UPLOAD
- ☐ EFFECTS
- ☐ MUSIC
- ☐ POSTED

TALK ABOUT

☐
☐
☐
☐
☐
☐
☐
☐
☐
☐

SOCIAL MEDIA

☐ ✉ ☐ 📷 ☐ f
☐ 🐦 ☐ P ☐ W

LINKS

YouTube *Planner*

VIDEO TITLE	CATEGORY	DURATION
KEYWORDS	📅	🕒

DESCRIPTION

SUPPLIES

CHECKLIST

- ☐ 🎥 FILM
- ☐ 🎤 VOICEOVER
- ☐ 📝 EDIT
- ☐ 🖼 THUMBNAIL
- ☐ 📄 DESCRIPTION
- ☐ 🏷 TAG
- ☐ 📤 UPLOAD
- ☐ ✨ EFFECTS
- ☐ 🎵 MUSIC
- ☐ 🎉 POSTED

TALK ABOUT

- ☐
- ☐
- ☐
- ☐
- ☐
- ☐
- ☐
- ☐
- ☐
- ☐
- ☐
- ☐

SOCIAL MEDIA

- ☐ ✉️
- ☐ 🐦
- ☐ 📷
- ☐ 📌
- ☐ f
- ☐ W

LINKS

YouTube *Planner*

VIDEO TITLE	CATEGORY	DURATION
KEYWORDS	📅	🕒

DESCRIPTION

SUPPLIES

CHECKLIST

- ☐ 🎥 FILM
- ☐ 🎤 VOICEOVER
- ☐ 📝 EDIT
- ☐ 🖼 THUMBNAIL
- ☐ 📄 DESCRIPTION
- ☐ 🏷 TAG
- ☐ ⬆ UPLOAD
- ☐ ✨ EFFECTS
- ☐ 🎵 MUSIC
- ☐ 🎉 POSTED

TALK ABOUT

- ☐
- ☐
- ☐
- ☐
- ☐
- ☐
- ☐
- ☐
- ☐
- ☐
- ☐
- ☐

SOCIAL MEDIA

- ☐ ✉
- ☐ 📷 Instagram
- ☐ f Facebook
- ☐ 🐦 Twitter
- ☐ 📌 Pinterest
- ☐ W WordPress

LINKS

YouTube *Planner*

VIDEO TITLE

CATEGORY

DURATION

KEYWORDS

DESCRIPTION

SUPPLIES

CHECKLIST

- [ ] FILM
- [ ] VOICEOVER
- [ ] EDIT
- [ ] THUMBNAIL
- [ ] DESCRIPTION
- [ ] TAG
- [ ] UPLOAD
- [ ] EFFECTS
- [ ] MUSIC
- [ ] POSTED

TALK ABOUT

SOCIAL MEDIA

- [ ] ✉
- [ ] Instagram
- [ ] Facebook
- [ ] Twitter
- [ ] Pinterest
- [ ] WordPress

LINKS

YouTube *Planner*

VIDEO TITLE	CATEGORY	DURATION
KEYWORDS		

DESCRIPTION

SUPPLIES

CHECKLIST

- ☐ FILM
- ☐ VOICEOVER
- ☐ EDIT
- ☐ THUMBNAIL
- ☐ DESCRIPTION
- ☐ TAG
- ☐ UPLOAD
- ☐ EFFECTS
- ☐ MUSIC
- ☐ POSTED

TALK ABOUT

SOCIAL MEDIA

- ☐ ✉
- ☐ Instagram
- ☐ Facebook
- ☐ Twitter
- ☐ Pinterest
- ☐ WordPress

LINKS

YouTube *Planner*

| VIDEO TITLE | CATEGORY | DURATION |
| KEYWORDS | 📅 | 🕐 |

DESCRIPTION

SUPPLIES

CHECKLIST

- [ ] 🎥 FILM
- [ ] 🎤 VOICEOVER
- [ ] 📝 EDIT
- [ ] 🖼 THUMBNAIL
- [ ] 📄 DESCRIPTION
- [ ] 🏷 TAG
- [ ] ⬆ UPLOAD
- [ ] ✨ EFFECTS
- [ ] 🎵 MUSIC
- [ ] 🎉 POSTED

TALK ABOUT

- [ ]
- [ ]
- [ ]
- [ ]
- [ ]
- [ ]
- [ ]
- [ ]
- [ ]
- [ ]
- [ ]
- [ ]

SOCIAL MEDIA

- [ ] ✉
- [ ] 📷
- [ ] f
- [ ] 🐦
- [ ] P
- [ ] W

LINKS

YouTube *Planner*

VIDEO TITLE	CATEGORY	DURATION
KEYWORDS		

DESCRIPTION

SUPPLIES

CHECKLIST

- ☐ FILM
- ☐ VOICEOVER
- ☐ EDIT
- ☐ THUMBNAIL
- ☐ DESCRIPTION
- ☐ TAG
- ☐ UPLOAD
- ☐ EFFECTS
- ☐ MUSIC
- ☐ POSTED

TALK ABOUT

- ☐
- ☐
- ☐
- ☐
- ☐
- ☐
- ☐
- ☐
- ☐
- ☐
- ☐

SOCIAL MEDIA

- ☐ ✉
- ☐ Instagram
- ☐ Facebook
- ☐ Twitter
- ☐ Pinterest
- ☐ WordPress

LINKS

YouTube *Planner*

| VIDEO TITLE | CATEGORY | DURATION |

KEYWORDS

DESCRIPTION

SUPPLIES

CHECKLIST

- [ ] FILM
- [ ] VOICEOVER
- [ ] EDIT
- [ ] THUMBNAIL
- [ ] DESCRIPTION
- [ ] TAG
- [ ] UPLOAD
- [ ] EFFECTS
- [ ] MUSIC
- [ ] POSTED

TALK ABOUT

- [ ]
- [ ]
- [ ]
- [ ]
- [ ]
- [ ]
- [ ]
- [ ]
- [ ]
- [ ]
- [ ]
- [ ]

SOCIAL MEDIA

- [ ] Email
- [ ] Instagram
- [ ] Facebook
- [ ] Twitter
- [ ] Pinterest
- [ ] WordPress

LINKS

YouTube *Planner*

| VIDEO TITLE | CATEGORY | DURATION |

KEYWORDS

DESCRIPTION

SUPPLIES

CHECKLIST

- [ ] FILM
- [ ] VOICEOVER
- [ ] EDIT
- [ ] THUMBNAIL
- [ ] DESCRIPTION
- [ ] TAG
- [ ] UPLOAD
- [ ] EFFECTS
- [ ] MUSIC
- [ ] POSTED

TALK ABOUT

SOCIAL MEDIA

- [ ] ✉
- [ ] Instagram
- [ ] Facebook
- [ ] Twitter
- [ ] Pinterest
- [ ] WordPress

LINKS

YouTube *Planner*

| VIDEO TITLE | CATEGORY | DURATION |
| KEYWORDS | 📅 | 🕐 |

DESCRIPTION

SUPPLIES

CHECKLIST

- ☐ 🎥 FILM
- ☐ 🎤 VOICEOVER
- ☐ 📝 EDIT
- ☐ 🖼 THUMBNAIL
- ☐ 📄 DESCRIPTION
- ☐ 🏷 TAG
- ☐ ⬆ UPLOAD
- ☐ ✨ EFFECTS
- ☐ 🎵 MUSIC
- ☐ 🎉 POSTED

TALK ABOUT

- ☐
- ☐
- ☐
- ☐
- ☐
- ☐
- ☐
- ☐
- ☐
- ☐
- ☐
- ☐

SOCIAL MEDIA

- ☐ ✉
- ☐ 📷
- ☐ f
- ☐ 🐦
- ☐ P
- ☐ Ⓦ

LINKS

YouTube *Planner*

VIDEO TITLE	CATEGORY	DURATION
KEYWORDS	📅	🕒

DESCRIPTION

SUPPLIES

CHECKLIST

- ☐ 🎥 FILM
- ☐ 🎤 VOICEOVER
- ☐ 📝 EDIT
- ☐ 🖼 THUMBNAIL
- ☐ 📄 DESCRIPTION
- ☐ 🏷 TAG
- ☐ ⬆ UPLOAD
- ☐ ✨ EFFECTS
- ☐ 🎵 MUSIC
- ☐ 🎉 POSTED

TALK ABOUT

- ☐
- ☐
- ☐
- ☐
- ☐
- ☐
- ☐
- ☐
- ☐
- ☐
- ☐

SOCIAL MEDIA

- ☐ ✉
- ☐ 📷 Instagram
- ☐ f Facebook
- ☐ 🐦 Twitter
- ☐ P Pinterest
- ☐ W WordPress

LINKS

YouTube *Planner*

VIDEO TITLE

CATEGORY

DURATION

KEYWORDS

DESCRIPTION

SUPPLIES

CHECKLIST

- ☐ 🎥 FILM
- ☐ 🎤 VOICEOVER
- ☐ 📝 EDIT
- ☐ 🖼 THUMBNAIL
- ☐ 📄 DESCRIPTION
- ☐ 🏷 TAG
- ☐ ⬆ UPLOAD
- ☐ ✨ EFFECTS
- ☐ 🎵 MUSIC
- ☐ 🎉 POSTED

TALK ABOUT

SOCIAL MEDIA

- ☐ ✉
- ☐ 📷
- ☐ f
- ☐ 🐦
- ☐ P
- ☐ W

LINKS

YouTube *Planner*

| VIDEO TITLE | CATEGORY | DURATION |

KEYWORDS

DESCRIPTION

SUPPLIES

CHECKLIST

- ☐ 🎥 FILM
- ☐ 🎤 VOICEOVER
- ☐ 📝 EDIT
- ☐ 🖼 THUMBNAIL
- ☐ 📄 DESCRIPTION
- ☐ 🏷 TAG
- ☐ ⬆ UPLOAD
- ☐ ✨ EFFECTS
- ☐ 🎵 MUSIC
- ☐ 🎉 POSTED

TALK ABOUT

- ☐
- ☐
- ☐
- ☐
- ☐
- ☐
- ☐
- ☐
- ☐
- ☐
- ☐
- ☐
- ☐

SOCIAL MEDIA

- ☐ ✉
- ☐ Instagram
- ☐ Facebook
- ☐ Twitter
- ☐ Pinterest
- ☐ WordPress

LINKS

YouTube *Planner*

VIDEO TITLE	CATEGORY	DURATION
KEYWORDS	📅	🕐

DESCRIPTION

SUPPLIES

CHECKLIST

- ☐ 🎥 FILM
- ☐ 🎤 VOICEOVER
- ☐ 📝 EDIT
- ☐ 🖼 THUMBNAIL
- ☐ 📄 DESCRIPTION
- ☐ 🏷 TAG
- ☐ ⬆ UPLOAD
- ☐ ✨ EFFECTS
- ☐ 🎵 MUSIC
- ☐ 🎉 POSTED

TALK ABOUT

- ☐
- ☐
- ☐
- ☐
- ☐
- ☐
- ☐
- ☐
- ☐
- ☐
- ☐
- ☐

SOCIAL MEDIA

- ☐ ✉
- ☐ 📷 Instagram
- ☐ f Facebook
- ☐ 🐦 Twitter
- ☐ P Pinterest
- ☐ Ⓦ WordPress

LINKS

YouTube *Planner*

VIDEO TITLE

CATEGORY

DURATION

KEYWORDS

DESCRIPTION

SUPPLIES

CHECKLIST

- ☐ FILM
- ☐ VOICEOVER
- ☐ EDIT
- ☐ THUMBNAIL
- ☐ DESCRIPTION
- ☐ TAG
- ☐ UPLOAD
- ☐ EFFECTS
- ☐ MUSIC
- ☐ POSTED

TALK ABOUT

SOCIAL MEDIA

- ☐ ✉
- ☐ Instagram
- ☐ Facebook
- ☐ Twitter
- ☐ Pinterest
- ☐ WordPress

LINKS

YouTube *Planner*

VIDEO TITLE	CATEGORY	DURATION
KEYWORDS	📅	🕒

DESCRIPTION

SUPPLIES

CHECKLIST

- ☐ 🎥 FILM
- ☐ 🎙 VOICEOVER
- ☐ 📝 EDIT
- ☐ 🖼 THUMBNAIL
- ☐ 📄 DESCRIPTION
- ☐ 🏷 TAG
- ☐ ⬆ UPLOAD
- ☐ ✨ EFFECTS
- ☐ 🎵 MUSIC
- ☐ 🎉 POSTED

TALK ABOUT

- ☐
- ☐
- ☐
- ☐
- ☐
- ☐
- ☐
- ☐
- ☐
- ☐
- ☐
- ☐

SOCIAL MEDIA

- ☐ ✉
- ☐ 📷 Instagram
- ☐ Facebook
- ☐ Twitter
- ☐ Pinterest
- ☐ WordPress

LINKS

YouTube *Planner*

| VIDEO TITLE | CATEGORY | DURATION |

KEYWORDS

DESCRIPTION

SUPPLIES

CHECKLIST

- ☐ FILM
- ☐ VOICEOVER
- ☐ EDIT
- ☐ THUMBNAIL
- ☐ DESCRIPTION
- ☐ TAG
- ☐ UPLOAD
- ☐ EFFECTS
- ☐ MUSIC
- ☐ POSTED

TALK ABOUT

SOCIAL MEDIA

LINKS

YouTube *Planner*

VIDEO TITLE	CATEGORY	DURATION
KEYWORDS	📅	🕐

DESCRIPTION

SUPPLIES

CHECKLIST

- ☐ 🎥 FILM
- ☐ 🎤 VOICEOVER
- ☐ 📝 EDIT
- ☐ 🖼 THUMBNAIL
- ☐ 📄 DESCRIPTION
- ☐ 🏷 TAG
- ☐ ⬆ UPLOAD
- ☐ ✨ EFFECTS
- ☐ 🎵 MUSIC
- ☐ 🎉 POSTED

TALK ABOUT

- ☐
- ☐
- ☐
- ☐
- ☐
- ☐
- ☐
- ☐
- ☐
- ☐
- ☐
- ☐

SOCIAL MEDIA

- ☐ ✉
- ☐ 📷 Instagram
- ☐ f Facebook
- ☐ 🐦 Twitter
- ☐ 📌 Pinterest
- ☐ Ⓦ WordPress

LINKS

YouTube *Planner*

VIDEO TITLE	CATEGORY	DURATION

KEYWORDS

DESCRIPTION

SUPPLIES

CHECKLIST

- [ ] FILM
- [ ] VOICEOVER
- [ ] EDIT
- [ ] THUMBNAIL
- [ ] DESCRIPTION
- [ ] TAG
- [ ] UPLOAD
- [ ] EFFECTS
- [ ] MUSIC
- [ ] POSTED

TALK ABOUT

- [ ]
- [ ]
- [ ]
- [ ]
- [ ]
- [ ]
- [ ]
- [ ]
- [ ]
- [ ]
- [ ]
- [ ]

SOCIAL MEDIA

- [ ] ✉
- [ ] Instagram
- [ ] Facebook
- [ ] Twitter
- [ ] Pinterest
- [ ] WordPress

LINKS

YouTube *Planner*

VIDEO TITLE

CATEGORY

DURATION

KEYWORDS

DESCRIPTION

SUPPLIES

CHECKLIST

- ☐ 🎥 FILM
- ☐ 🎤 VOICEOVER
- ☐ 📝 EDIT
- ☐ 🖼 THUMBNAIL
- ☐ 📄 DESCRIPTION
- ☐ 🏷 TAG
- ☐ ⬆ UPLOAD
- ☐ ✨ EFFECTS
- ☐ 🎵 MUSIC
- ☐ 🎉 POSTED

TALK ABOUT

☐
☐
☐
☐
☐
☐
☐
☐
☐
☐
☐

SOCIAL MEDIA

☐ ✉ ☐ 📷 ☐ f
☐ 🐦 ☐ P ☐ W

LINKS

YouTube *Planner*

| VIDEO TITLE | CATEGORY | DURATION |

KEYWORDS

DESCRIPTION

SUPPLIES

CHECKLIST

- ☐ FILM
- ☐ VOICEOVER
- ☐ EDIT
- ☐ THUMBNAIL
- ☐ DESCRIPTION
- ☐ TAG
- ☐ UPLOAD
- ☐ EFFECTS
- ☐ MUSIC
- ☐ POSTED

TALK ABOUT

- ☐
- ☐
- ☐
- ☐
- ☐
- ☐
- ☐
- ☐
- ☐
- ☐
- ☐

SOCIAL MEDIA

- ☐ ✉
- ☐ Instagram
- ☐ Facebook
- ☐ Twitter
- ☐ Pinterest
- ☐ WordPress

LINKS

YouTube *Planner*

| VIDEO TITLE | CATEGORY | DURATION |
| KEYWORDS | 📅 | 🕐 |

DESCRIPTION

SUPPLIES

CHECKLIST

- [ ] 🎥 FILM
- [ ] 🎤 VOICEOVER
- [ ] 📝 EDIT
- [ ] 🖼 THUMBNAIL
- [ ] 📄 DESCRIPTION
- [ ] 🏷 TAG
- [ ] ⬆ UPLOAD
- [ ] ✨ EFFECTS
- [ ] 🎵 MUSIC
- [ ] 🎉 POSTED

TALK ABOUT

- [ ]
- [ ]
- [ ]
- [ ]
- [ ]
- [ ]
- [ ]
- [ ]
- [ ]
- [ ]
- [ ]

SOCIAL MEDIA

- [ ] ✉
- [ ] 📷 Instagram
- [ ] f Facebook
- [ ] 🐦 Twitter
- [ ] 📌 Pinterest
- [ ] Ⓦ WordPress

LINKS

YouTube *Planner*

VIDEO TITLE	CATEGORY	DURATION
KEYWORDS	📅	🕐

DESCRIPTION

SUPPLIES

CHECKLIST

- ☐ 🎥 FILM
- ☐ 🎤 VOICEOVER
- ☐ 📝 EDIT
- ☐ 🖼 THUMBNAIL
- ☐ 📄 DESCRIPTION
- ☐ 🏷 TAG
- ☐ ⬆ UPLOAD
- ☐ ✨ EFFECTS
- ☐ 🎵 MUSIC
- ☐ 🎉 POSTED

TALK ABOUT

- ☐
- ☐
- ☐
- ☐
- ☐
- ☐
- ☐
- ☐
- ☐
- ☐

SOCIAL MEDIA

- ☐ ✉
- ☐ 📷 Instagram
- ☐ f Facebook
- ☐ 🐦 Twitter
- ☐ P Pinterest
- ☐ W WordPress

LINKS

Printed in Great Britain
by Amazon